HALTON
AND THE APPRENTICE SCHEME

Midland Publishing
Limited

Photographs on the cover:

Front: **By the early 1960s Hunters had become the predominant training type as members of the 91st Entry (January 1959 to December 1961) learn ejection seat safety precautions. The Hunter F.4 7510M was serialled WT694.** via HAAA

Back cover, top: **Jet Provosts and Jaguars in use at Halton in the New Workshops in September 1987** (Author)

Back cover, bottom: **The arrival of Jaguars in the 1990s provided Halton with the opportunity to provide training on aircraft representative of the RAF's current front line.** via HAAA

Opposite: **Lord Trenchard inspects the graduation parade at Halton on 25th July 1933. He is accompanied by Air Commodore I M Bonham-Carter (at the rear of Trenchard)** via HAAA

HALTON

AND THE APPRENTICE SCHEME

Bill Taylor

This book
is respectfully dedicated to
Trenchard's Brats

Copyright 1993
Bill Taylor
and Midland Publishing Limited

Published by
Midland Publishing Limited
24, The Hollow, Earl Shilton
Leicester, LE9 7NA
England

ISBN 0-85780-015-X

Printed in England by
The Nuffield Press Limited
Cowley, Oxford
OX9 1TR

Typeset
in ITC Cheltenham
and Swiss

Designed by
Midland Publishing
and Stephen Thompson Associates

FOREWORD

On the 24th June 1993, the graduation of the 155 Entry of Aircraft Apprentices brought 73 years of Royal Air Force Aircraft Apprentice training at Royal Air Force Halton to a close. The occasion was marked by a Royal Review of the graduation by HRH The Duke of Gloucester.

The Lord Trenchard, as part of his vision to train an elite of engineers in a wide variety of trades for aircraft maintenance, established No.1 School of Technical Training at Royal Air force Halton in 1920. Although the School has trained many airmen on a variety of courses, the mainstay of the School has been the Aircraft Apprentice Training which has long enjoyed world-wide recognition as one of the best technical training schemes available for young men seeking a career in aircraft engineering. The graduates of the Scheme have a justifiable reputation for high technical ability, initiative and sound character and many have reached eminent positions in the Royal Air Force, many foreign air forces and in the aerospace industry both at home and abroad. It is sad to see the end of a scheme that has served the Royal Air Force so well for so long.

Royal Air Force Halton has been the home of aircraft engineering training for over 70 years. However, the changing needs of the Royal Air Force over recent years necessitated a rationalisation of training facilities and, as a result, No.1 School of Technical Training is to relocate to Royal Air Force Cosford during 1993-94 to form the centre of excellence for all aircraft engineering training and thus maintain the historic link between Trenchard and engineering training. At the same time, Royal Air Force Halton will be developed into a centre of excellence for recruit training and the training of the administration, supply and security disciplines.

I am delighted that my colleague Group Captain Bill Taylor has taken the trouble to research the history of Royal Air Force Halton and the Apprenticeship Scheme and write this most comprehensive book to mark the end of an era in Royal Air Force history.

G O Burton

Group Captain G O Burton RAF
Officer Commanding
No.1 School of Technical Training
and Royal Air Force Halton.

INTRODUCTION

After seventy three distinguished years the Royal Air Force's Apprentice Scheme came to an end in 1993. Conceived by Lord Trenchard in his vision for the fledgling RAF, the Apprentice Scheme began in January 1920 when the first entry of Boy Mechanics arrived to start their training at Cranwell. The title Aircraft Apprentice was introduced to replace Boy Mechanic in 1922 on the arrival of the first apprentices at Halton, following the construction of permanent accommodation.

Since then, Halton has become inextricably linked with excellence in aircraft engineering. Moreover, the three years an Aircraft Apprentice spent at Halton saw his transition from youth to adult. Under the careful stewardship of the RAF, each apprentice extended his education and had his character developed. This mechanism was an investment for the future which was to be repaid manifold because the expansion of the RAF from the mid-1930s was founded on the skill and character of the Halton product.

It is therefore fitting that in the year in which the last RAF apprentices enter operational service, and Halton begins to lose its engineering training function, a book should be published to mark the end of a pillar on which Lord Trenchard founded the peacetime RAF. It is difficult, if not impossible, to encapsulate every aspect of seventy three years of the Halton Tradition in such a small space. I can but hope that this small effort does justice to such a mighty subject.

Moreover, researching and writing the narrative for this book, and writing the captions for the photographs, has underlined to me the importance of recording the detailed history of Halton and all aspects of the Apprentice Scheme. Perhaps this work will be seen as a small step along the way towards production of the definitive history of the Scheme in 1995. With the focus provided by the Halton Aircraft Apprentices Association, I am sure that it will.

Bill Taylor
Friskney, Boston   May 1993

ACKNOWLEDGEMENTS

The compilation and production of this book could not have been achieved so quickly without the ready support and assistance of many people. Fundamental to the photographic content has been the ready support of the Chairman of the Halton Aircraft Apprentices Association, Air Commodore Mike Evans; the HAAA's Archivist, Joe Ainsworth, and Secretary Alan Small. Considerable support was also provided by RAF Halton, under the command of Group Captain G. O. Burton RAF, himself an exapprentice of the 100th Entry. The total support and commitment of Squadron Leader Ken Clifford MBE, the Officer Commanding Apprentice Training Squadron, and his staff was vital to achieving the tight production timescale. Colin 'Oscar' Smedley has worked his usual miracles with some negatives of rather dubious quality. As usual, Chris Ashworth, Peter Green, Paddy Porter and Bruce Robertson have rallied to the call and Chris Salter has given help and advice on the production side at Earl Shilton. Thank you all.

Description: In front of a wreath of laurel five arrows one in pale the others in saltire barbs downwards surmounted fess wise of a propeller.

Motto: 'Teach Learn Apply'

Authority: Queen Elizabeth II, October 1981.

Promulgation: DCI 276/81

Derivation: Halton was first used as a military site in 1913 and has been in continuous use since then; the first RAF Commanding Officer was appointed in 1919. In allusion to the station's history going back to the beginning of the RAF, the Station has chosen a wooden propeller superimposed on five arrows, the latter being contained in the Arms of the Rothschild family to whom the estate originally belonged, the whole set in front of a laurel wreath denoting the experience of the work at all of the units on the station. The Motto 'Teach Learn Apply' signifies the work of the units since each has a training role in addition to its other functions.

Description: On a Mound, a Beech Tree.

Motto: 'Crescentes Discimus' (Growing We Learn, or As We Grow We Learn).

Authority: King George VI, June 1939.

Promulgation: AMO N674/39

Derivation: The Badge incorporates a symbolic tree of learning in the form of a beech tree. The beech tree was chosen as a reference to the site of the School being overlooked by a beechwood.

THE RAF HALTON
AIRCRAFT APPRENTICES ASSOCIATION

On the occasion of the Diamond Jubilee Reunion of Aircraft Apprentices at Halton in September 1980 it was agreed to form an association to foster the comradeship between all ex-Halton apprentices, to maintain contacts and to organise reunions. The HAAA was quickly formed and now flourishes, with membership now approaching 4,000.

Members are kept in touch by means of regular Newsletters and the Association's own Journal, *The Haltonian*, which is published twice a year. Additionally, the HAAA organises the Triennial Reunion at Halton and there are Area and individual Entry Branches which organise regular local meetings and periodic get-togethers. The HAAA is also active in the welfare of ex-apprentices.

Membership of the HAAA is open to all RAF Aircraft Apprentices, Technician Apprentices, Craft Apprentices and Royal Navy Artificer Apprentices (Air) who underwent all or part of their training at Halton, including their predecessor Boy Mechanics and apprentices from The Commonwealth Air Forces. Membership is also open to those who were trained in the early entries at Cranwell. The HAAA maintains an office at Halton which will be retained despite the departure of the RAF's engineering training to Cosford.

Former Halton Apprentices may obtain details of the HAAA from:

The Secretary
RAF Halton Aircraft Apprentices Assoc.
Royal Air Force
Halton
Aylesbury, Buckinghamshire
HP22 5PG

The RAF Halton Aircraft Apprentices Association is registered under the Charities Act, 1960, No.292523.

HALTON
AND THE APPRENTICE SCHEME

The Graduation Parade of the 155th Entry of Apprentice Engineering Technicians at No 1 School of Technical Training on 24th June 1993, marked the departure of Halton's last entry of apprentices. With the graduation of the 155th Entry from Cosford's No 2 School of Technical Training on 7th October 1993, Trenchard's Aircraft Apprentice Scheme ended.

On the 11th November 1919, when Trenchard submitted his paper founding the peacetime Royal Air Force, the total number of aircraft on charge in the RAF was 22,647. A new concept of war had been created in a new dimension and the RAF had come to stay. With the recognition of this came a host of new problems, not least of which was the need to train personnel in a wide variety of engineering trades, especially those associated with aircraft maintenance. Experience in civilian life had proved that the best way to produce a skilled man was to train him from youth in the environment he would eventually work in as a man - in other words, an apprenticeship.

In formulating his ideas for aircraft technical training in the peacetime RAF, Trenchard had inherited a long tradition of boys service dating back long before the First World War, both in the Royal Navy and in the Army. Rapid expansion of the Royal Flying Corps during the war had generated a shortage of skilled mechanics, forty-seven of whom were needed to support one front-line aircraft. In the early stages of the war the stream of volunteers entering the Army was combed for the skilled men needed to maintain the RFC's aeroplanes. However, it was quickly realised that the fledgling air army would have to train its own mechanics if the shortage was to be overcome.

Prior to the outbreak of war, the technical training of men was carried out at the Central Flying School, Netheravon. With the growing demand for specialist skills, a number of additional schools were established. Whilst the CFS took 200 trainees, No 1 School of Instruction at Reading held 1,000 and, from 27th October 1916, a converted jam factory at nearby Coley Park held 2,000. A further 300 men were also being trained in a former factory in Edinburgh. Moreover, there was no basic engineering course for semi-skilled recruits and 400 men were therefore sent to polytechnics for training. This kind of improvisation could not provide the men the RFC needed and rationalisation of the training machine became an urgent need.

Development at Halton

Attention turned to the Rothschild estate at Halton Park, near Wendover in Buckinghamshire, which was first used by the Army for summer manoeuvres in September 1913. The Army was joined at Halton by No 3 Squadron, RFC, under the command of Major Henry Brooke-Popham, with a handful of frail machines. With the outbreak of hostilities, Alfred Rothschild offered use of the estate to the Army, whilst his brother Nathaniel offered use of the adjoining Aston Clinton estate also. Tents were rapidly pitched over the estate, many on the site of the present airfield, and in September 1914 some 12,000 men of the 21st Yorkshire Division began to arrive.

During the succeeding winter a large number of wooden hutments were erected on three sites; North Camp held 5,000 men, East Camp another 5,000 and West Camp 2,000. After completing its military training, the 21st Division set off for the trenches of France, the first men starting from Halton on 15th August 1915. The East Anglians followed the 21st to Halton and soon more than 200 acres of Halton Park had been swallowed up by the Army. However, by the end of 1916 Halton had lost its divisional status and the first RFC unit, a recruit training centre arrived.

With the pressing need to expand technical training in the RFC, in June 1917, General Sir Sefton Brancker, Deputy Director General of Military Aeronautics, submitted proposals to centralise the technical training of men, women and boys in a new school to be located at Halton. In July 1917, the sum of £100,000 was allocated for the construction of permanent workshops to house the RFC's many trade specialities. The Army departed from Halton in the summer of 1917 and fitters and riggers of the RFC arrived from Reading on 20th August and 10th September respectively. Named the School of Technical Training (Men), the new school was under the direct control of the War Office and was commanded by Lieutenant Colonel Ian Bonham-Carter. Halton's population was huge, the camp having grown to house 6,000 airmen mechanics, 2,000 boys at the Boys Training Depot, West Camp, plus a further 1,700 instructors and other staff. Another 2,000 women were also under training in a variety of aircraft trades. There was also a lodger unit of the Australian Flying Corps which set up a training and supply depot at the East Camp in September 1917.

At first the training facilities were poor. However, by November the foundations of the huge new workshops had been laid and construction progressed rapidly, being carried out by a large labour force including a number of German prisoners of war. The workshops block covered 300,000 square feet, each of the twelve bays being 50 ft wide and 500 ft long. Designed to accommodate a different trade specialisation in each bay, the

workshop bays were taken over one by one on their completion so that training could get underway as quickly as possible. The throughput was large, and despite the spartan facilities Halton churned out no less than 14,000 mechanics in 1917 alone.

Whilst all this was happening, it was realised that the grounds at Halton were not owned by the War Office. Under the terms of Alfred Rothschild's offer of 1914, the new Service would have to vacate the estate within six months of the end of hostilities, returning it to the owner in the same condition in which it was lent. Clearly, after such widespread construction over so many acres, the cost of rehabilitation would be huge. The only answer was purchase and the Air Board drew up plans to buy the Halton estate. In addition to it being the location of the technical training school, the Air Board also envisaged that the large estate would eventually house the Staff College, the Cadet College, or perhaps also become the RAF's new permanent Depot.

However, the War Office was more cautious in its approach to the Treasury, seeking approval in December 1917 to purchase just 1,340 acres of the estate at a maximum sum of £50,000. Unfortunately, the War Office bid was rejected and on 31st January 1918, Alfred Rothschild died. Subsequent negotiations with Major Lionel Nathan de Rothschild finally resulted in Treasury approval to purchase all 3,014 acres of the estate, including the mansion, Halton village, the lodges and farms and fixtures and machinery, for a total of £112,000. The transaction was clearly a

Above left: **Hundreds of tents and many huts were erected to accommodate the Army units in Halton Park, as seen in this sunset view in 1914.** via HAAA

Left: **The front entrance of the newly-built Workshops building in 1918, shortly after completion. Inscriptions on the doors, including Acetylene Welding Shop and Coppersmiths and Tinsmiths Shop on the first two bays, proclaim the task of each bay.** via HAAA

bargain because the probate value of the estate was at least £360,000. Agreement to the terms was reached on 28th May 1918, and the Air Ministry took over the mansion on September 29th, after the Rothschild family had moved out. From 1919, Halton House became the Officers' Mess, with the house and its grounds being partially refurbished by German prisoners of war.

Training Rationalisation

Returning to the efforts of the RFC to rationalise its training, the S of TT (Men) had been located at Halton with effect from 10th September, 1917, with the training of boys kept separate from that of the men in a Boys Training Depot. Further boys training establishments were formed at Eastchurch and Letchworth and a Boys Training Wing was formed at Cranwell. The boys training establishments at Cranwell and Halton were retained for use by the post-war Air Force and on 9th September 1919, the School of Technical Training (Boys) was formed at Halton, although it did not take up its new title until 23rd December. In March 1920 the title of the school was changed to No 1 School of Technical Training (Boys), Halton, whilst at the same time the Boys Training Wing at Cranwell was renamed No 2 School of Technical Training (Boys), Cranwell.

Changes in boys training were subsequently brought about by Trenchard's vision of the permanent RAF, which was published in November 1919 and endorsed by Churchill, the Secretary of State for Air, the following month. Trenchard saw that the only way to recruit the high quality mechanics for the ever-more technical service was to train them internally. It was Trenchard's view that the fledgling RAF could not hope to compete with the civil market for skilled men who had served full apprenticeships and who could therefore command good wages. He proposed that as far as possible, all technical trades should be filled by recruiting boys between the ages of fifteen and sixteen years for courses in workshop training, together with technical and general educa-

tion, and to develop this scheme based on an apprenticeship of three years. He saw the added benefit that such training would also foster a spirit in the RAF on which so much was to depend in the future.

The Aircraft Apprentice Scheme

The Aircraft Apprentice Scheme was promulgated to Local Education Authorities in October 1919 and selection examinations were held in London and at fourteen provincial centres. The first 235 boys were accepted for a three-year apprenticeship although they began their training at Cranwell in January 1920 because permanent accommodation was still being built at Halton. Another 242 boys arrived at Cranwell in September 1920 and it was not until the 5th entry in January 1922 that apprentices arrived at Halton. The move to Halton coincided with adoption of the rank of Aircraft Apprentice for the boys, rather than the earlier title Boy Mechanic, and in May 1922 the scheme of appointing apprentices to their own Apprentice NCO ranks was also introduced. However, apprentice training also continued at Cranwell, with 981 boys under training there in 1924, long after Halton had opened, until the summer of 1926 when all but the electrical and wireless trades were transferred from Cranwell to Halton.

Halton House, photographed in 1937, shortly before the conservatory or Winter Garden on the left of the magnificent Rothschild mansion was demolished to make way for an accommodation block for the Officers' Mess. via HAAA

At the heart of Trenchard's vision was the recruitment of well-educated boys, because he saw ex-apprentices going on to form almost 40% of the RAF's groundcrew and more than 60% of its skilled tradesmen. It was thought that the selected boys, because of their resourcefulness and intelligence, could rapidly absorb the necessary technical training, and thereby complete their apprenticeship in three years rather than the normal five years in civil life, with a considerable saving in cost. The planned intake was about a 1,000 per year, and practical experience of the scheme soon gave concrete support to Trenchard's argument.

On arrival at Halton, the boys were medically examined and then 'signed-on' for twelve years' service from the age of 18. After attestation, the new apprentices were allocated to one of the principal trades of 'Fitter', 'Carpenter', 'Sheet Metal Worker' or 'Electrical'. The principal trades were further sub-divided into particular specialisations, such as the Fitter Aero Engines, or the Fitter

Armourer. By the end of the 1920s, the trade of Rigger (Metal) had been introduced to prepare apprentices for work on the new generation of all-metal aeroplanes then under development. The majority of apprentices began their training at Halton, although those destined for the electrical trade went to Flowerdown, near Winchester. Having been allotted to a trade and kitted out, apprentices were also allotted to a Section (later to become a Wing), which served to sub-divide into more manageable elements the huge organisation that had grown out of the former Rothschild estate.

The key distinguishing feature of the apprentice has long been the Apprentice Badge or the well-known coloured headbands. That renowned token of the apprentice, the Apprentice Badge or 'Wheel', stems from 1918 when it was considered that the boys needed a badge to distinguish them from the men 'so as to check smoking and the foregathering of boys with men'. The design, which comprises a four-bladed propeller contained within a circlet, was authorised by Air Ministry Order 500, dated 17th April 1919, having been adopted in December 1918. Manufactured in brass, so that it could be highly polished

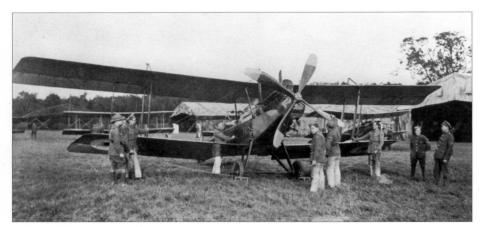

Left: **Trainees of the RFC and Australian Flying Corps receive instruction in engine starting at Halton Park in 1918. The aircraft is R.E.8 B7834.** via Bruce Robertson

Below: **The new barracks at Halton were first named Bulback Barracks, after the name of the wooded area to the centre right of the picture. Later, the barracks to the left were named Henderson whilst those to the right, at a more advanced stage of construction, were named Groves. The photograph was taken in about 1921.** via HAAA

every day, the badge was worn on the sleeve of the left arm, and has served as the Apprentice Badge ever since. There was, however, a break in use of the badge for a period of some ten years up to 1983, when its restoration was secured.

Similarly, a feature of the Apprentice Scheme at all of the schools has been the distinctive coloured headband worn with Service head-dress. As Halton built-up to its full strength, it quickly became apparent that some quick and easy means was required to identify apprentices to their parent Wing, or Section as the Wings were at first termed. The request was addressed to the Air Ministry by the Commandant, Air Commodore F R Scarlett CB DSO, and was approved in September 1920. In later years, coloured discs matching the headband were also displayed behind the RAF Badge on the beret and behind the Apprentice Badge on the sleeve. For a time in the early 1920s, apprentices also wore a brass numeral attached to the Crown on their cap badge to indicate their Wing.

Perhaps the most delicate of anecdotes is that which surrounds use of the name 'Brat'. There are a number of tales about the origin of this term, some more charitable than others. Perhaps the most plausible explanation is that as Trenchard's proteges began to filter out into the RAF at large, many of the existing tradesmen called them Trenchard Brats, at first as a term of derision in the true meaning of the word, a troublesome child. However, as time passed and the ex-apprentices were able to prove their worth, the term Brat soon became a name to be proud of.

Pattern of Training

Having started his training, the newly arrived apprentice quickly found his life falling into a well-ordered routine. Of the working week, twenty hours were devoted to technical training in the workshops, nine to physical training, drill and games, and eight to education. The remaining time was filled with barrack duties, inspections and preparation for technical or education subjects.

Above: **The 5th entry of Carpenter Riggers. These were the first Carpenter Riggers to arrive at Halton and commenced training in January 1922.** via HAAA

Recreational facilities were available in abundance, including a debating society and model aircraft club in addition to a wide variety of sporting facilities.

At the end of the first year's work there was an intermediate examination in educational subjects, followed by the final examinations at the end of the eighth term. Final examinations in skill-of-hand and trade knowledge were carried out in the last term. The marks obtained in the examinations would be used to determine the graduation rank and pay of the apprentice whilst those who were highest in the Order of Merit would also be considered for Cadetships to the Cadet College at Cranwell; Trenchard expected that ex-apprentices would provide up to 20% of the cadets on each Cranwell entry.

Technical training in the workshops came under the control of the Senior Technical Officer, and the technical staff included officers, NCO instructors and civilian instructors, a traditional mixture which continued to the end. The workshops were divided into two main departments, the Fitters' Shop and the Carpenters' Shop. Aircraft Apprentices were allocated to the various trades depending upon the vacancies available, whilst the pref-

erence of individuals and the results of the qualifying examinations were also taken into account. The trade of Wireless Operator was seen as the most important and the top forty of each apprentice entry was sent to Flowerdown for this training.

The first year of technical training on the course was given over almost entirely to basic training, such as the use of hand-tools and skill-of-hand, whilst those apprentices destined to be Carpenter Riggers spent their first year training in basic carpentry. Following basic training the apprentices took up their specialist trades for advanced training and within the overall Fitter trades, the trade of Fitter Aero Engine was assessed as the most important, followed by Fitter Driver Petrol and Fitter Armourer. However, it was found that by the end of basic training, some of the apprentices did not meet the standards of knowledge and skill required for their selected trade, and from October 1924 the allocation to trades was not made until

Aircraft Apprentice M Tillman, of the 16th Entry. Note the Apprentice Badge, the Bandsman Badge, and the number 4 behind the cap badge. via HAAA

the workshops. In 1924, the Records Office was extended and converted into the Schools building, now known as Kermode Hall. Also during 1924, two Flight Sheds were erected at the aerodrome, both of which were reputed to have been brought from France. The pace of construction continued unabated and additional barrack areas were built on the site of the Old Hospital.

Halton's own Aeroplane

The Halton Light Aeroplane Club, inspired by the success of a similar club at Cranwell under the direction of Flight Lieutenant N Comper, was founded in December 1925 with Flying Officer C H Latimer-Needham, an Education Officer at Halton, as its organising secretary and treasurer. Having viewed the contestants in the Daily Mail and Air Ministry light aeroplane trials of 1923-24, Latimer-Needham analysed the features of each type to produce a new design which incorporated the best of the features. Design work began at the end of 1924 and was completed by the end of 1925 in time for the launch of the club, which later became the Halton Aero Club. Construction began with the aid and support of the apprentices and instructional staff in February 1926, with the aim of completing the aircraft within six months. Unfortunately, the aircraft was not ready in time for the trials at Lympne in August 1926, and the HAC-1 'Mayfly', powered by a 32 hp Bristol Cherub III engine, was flown for the first time from Bicester by Flight Lieutenant C F le Poer Trench on 1st February 1927. After satisfactorily completing its test flights, the Mayfly was registered G-EBOO. After some success in flying meetings during 1927, it was decided to optimise the little biplane for air racing. Whilst a number of useful improvements in performance had been achieved, it was felt that the aircraft should be converted from its biplane configuration to that of a parasol monoplane. This was done over the winter of 1927/28 and the aircraft was renamed the HAC-2 'Minus'. After further success in the 1928 and 1929 flying meetings, the Minus was damaged during participation in the 1929

King's Cup air race; it was later dismantled and its registration mark cancelled in 1931.

However, that was not the end of the activities of the Halton Aero Club. The lower wings removed from the Mayfly during its conversion in 1927 were used by Flying Officer John Clarke, an ex-apprentice and ex-Cranwell cadet, to become the lower wings of an aircraft he designed using parts from a number of other aircraft, called the Clarke Cheetah (G-AAJK). Tragically, Clarke was killed when his Siskin hit a shed during take-off from Brough on 11th October 1929, just a month after the Cheetah gained its Certificate of Airworthiness. Latimer-Needham had been involved in the Cheetah project, providing design advice. He also provided advice to the Granger brothers of Nottingham, who designed and built the Archaeopteryx, a tailless design which was first flown in October 1930.

This activity spurred Latimer-Needham's interest in the tailless aircraft and he designed the HAC-3 Meteor in such a configuration, to be powered by two Cherub III engines mounted in push/pull configuration. However, when the project was 90% complete it was abandoned on official orders due to the move away from wooden construction in the RAF. Design work on the Meteor had been completed in 1928 and Latimer-Needham went on to design a successor, the HAC-4, which was to have been a six-seat cabin monoplane powered by three Cherub engines. However, with the rundown of the club's activities, design work on the HAC-4 was never completed and the Halton Aero Club was gradually transformed into the Halton Branch of the Royal Aeronautical Society, which continues to flourish today. Latimer-Needham went on to develop his interest in gliding and later he founded the Luton Aeroplane Co, designing such aircraft as the Luton Buzzard, the Luton Minor and the Luton Major.

Evolution of Training

As the pace of aircraft design and development accelerated, so the various apprentice

the end of basic training. As the first entry of Halton apprentices reached the end of its training, it was fitting that the Reviewing Officer at the Graduation Parade on 17th December 1924, should be Air Chief Marshal Sir Hugh Trenchard, Chief of the Air Staff.

As Halton settled down to its new role, work began to heal the wounds inflicted on the landscape of the estate by the wartime Army occupation and the massive construction programme for the RAF. Large areas of ground were cleared and great expanses of woodland were planted and some outlying portions of the estate were sold. However, the pace of construction did not relent. The Bulback Barracks area was constructed to house the burgeoning apprentice population and a Records Office was built adjacent to

training courses were adapted to meet the new challenge. In 1926 the training of Motor Body Builders ceased whilst, in 1927, the 16th Entry was the first to include training for metal riggers. Another hangar was erected on the aerodrome for use during the Flight Training element of the course, which was aimed at providing training in the handling of aircraft and aircraft operations, as required by the squadrons. Halton's medical capability was expanded considerably on 31st October 1927, when Her Royal Highness Princess Mary, Viscountess Lascelles, opened the Princess Mary's RAF Hospital.

In May 1928, Halton's barrack areas were named after important military figures. Henderson Barracks, occupied by No 1 Wing, was named after Lieutenant General Sir David Henderson, KCB KCVO DSO, who was the first Chairman of the RFC in 1912 and was the first commander of the RFC element of the British Expeditionary Force in France. He later became the General Officer Commanding the RFC and after the war he controlled the International Red Cross Organisation in Geneva until his death in 1921. No 2 Wing occupied Groves Barracks, named after Air Commodore R M Groves, CB DSO AFC, who served in the Naval Wing of the RFC, which in 1914 became the Royal Naval Air Service. In 1916 Groves became Assistant Secretary to the Air Board and in 1918 he became Deputy Chief of the Air Staff, under Trenchard. He was killed when a Bristol Fighter he was flying crashed in Egypt.

The barracks occupied by No 4 Wing was renamed Maitland Barracks on 28th July 1928, having been previously known as Chiltern Barracks. Air Commodore E M Maitland, CMG DSO AFC, was Commandant of the Howden airship station and an exponent of ballooning, airships and parachuting. He was killed in the crash of the airship R-38 on 24th August 1921. Shepherd Barracks were named after Brigadier General G S Shepherd MC, who commanded 6 Squadron

In a model of precision, the apprentices parade on 11th November 1924 for the Armistice Day memorial service. via HAAA

Top: **A variety of redundant airframes have served as training aids throughout Halton's existence. In the background can be seen a Sopwith Snipe carrying the instructional airframe serial number 168M.** via HAAA

Centre: **A pleasant scene as apprentices undergo their 'Drome Course', in which the skills of aircraft handling and engine running were taught.** via HAAA

Bottom: **The HAC-1 'Mayfly' nearing completion in the workshops, prior to its first flight and allocation of its civil registration, G-EBOO.** via HAAA

in France and rose to command 1 Brigade, also in France, in 1917. Built in the expansion period, Halton's fifth barrack area was named Paine Barracks after Captain, later Rear Admiral Sir Godfrey M Paine, CB MVO RN, who was appointed Commodore of the First Class in charge of the RNAS Central Depot and Training Establishment. On 13th December 1915, a hulk on the Medway was commissioned HMS Daedalus and Commodore Paine's Pennant was flown for just one day before being transferred to the new air station at Cranwell where Commodore Paine took command. He later went on to be the first Commandant of the Central Flying School and Inspector General of the RAF.

From 1933 it was decided to train apprentices in the combined trade of Fitter Aero Engine and Metal Rigger, in a new trade to be called Fitter II. A twelve-month conversion course was also begun in March that year to qualify existing single-skill tradesmen in the new multiple skills, but in 1935 it was moved to Henlow to free accommodation at Halton for the enlarged apprentice intake anticipated as part of the expansion of the RAF. Expansion brought with it nine new barrack blocks on Paine Wing and a substantial increase in entry size. Having started at around 500 in number in the early 1920s, entry size had dwindled to little more than 200 in the early 1930s. However, with the arrival of the 31st Entry in January 1935 with 551 recruits, numbers rapidly increased. The

32nd arrived in August 1935 with an intake of 916 and the 34th a year later had 1,250.

Pre-War Expansion

As the pace of the expansion gathered momentum, the RAF realised the desperate need to train substantial numbers of maintenance personnel. A site for a new school was chosen at Cosford, near Wolverhampton, and construction began in 1937. The Cosford school was first ready for occupation the following year, and it opened in August 1938 with a complement of two apprentice training wings and one wing for airmen training. No 5 (Apprentice) Wing from Halton was moved to Cosford on 4th August to act as an experienced nucleus for the new school and in December that year the Fitter Armourers also moved from Halton to Cosford. During 1939, a number of Naval apprentices arrived at Halton for training, to be supplemented by the transfer of a number of RAF apprentices to the Fleet Air Arm.

The flood of volunteers for apprentice training in the years before the war led to a blockage in the call-forward of recruits for training. As a result, the Air Ministry introduced the Boy Entrant Scheme for boys with lower academic ability than those selected for apprentice training. The new scheme included a twelve to fifteen-month course of training and revised terms of service. The first Boy Entrants began training as Wireless Operators at the Electrical and Wireless School, Cranwell, in September 1934 and the first Boy Entrant course for armourers began the same month at Eastchurch. However, with the outbreak of war, the training of Boy Entrants was suspended, until its reintroduction in May 1947.

Wartime Activity

With war looking ever more certain, in 1939 the length of the apprentice course was reduced from three to two and a half years. In December it was decided to reduce the course to two years duration and from 1940 the size of the apprentice entries was reduced to free accommodation, instructors

Above: **The delightful facade of the Princess Mary's Royal Air Force Hospital, sadly now hidden from direct view by newer buildings erected following the Second World War.** via HAAA

Below: **Members of the 43rd Entry, who arrived at Halton in August 1941, march away from an impressive line-up of aircraft parked in front of the New Workshops (blanked out by the censor) in 1943.** via HAAA

The Pipe Band and Lewis I parade on a wet day in 1945. via HAAA

and equipment for short, intensive training courses for airmen. However, with some foresight, from the arrival of the 47th Entry in August 1943, the three-year apprentice course was reinstated. That year also saw the introduction of an apprentice course for electricians.

Even with a war in progress, the aircraft apprenticeship scheme was still seen as a valuable start to a rewarding career. Trades open to the apprentice at the time included Fitter, Fitter (Armourer), Wireless Operator, Electrician and, finally, Instrument Maker. Apprentices would graduate at the end of their course in the rank of Leading Aircraftman, Aircraftman First Class or Aircraftman Second Class, depending upon their marks in the final examinations. There were normally two entries per year, in February and August, and one month before the end of their course all apprentices were given the opportunity to apply for training as airmen pilots, with the final selection being made in their third year after graduation. On satisfactory completion of flying training, ex-apprentices would be promoted to the rank of sergeant and on completion of six years flying, they would normally revert to their former trade, whilst retaining the rank.

The training and future employment of the aircraft apprentice afforded tremendous variety to the new recruit. During the first part of the course, basic trade knowledge and skill-of-hand was developed whilst the second part of the course applied this skill and knowledge to the specific requirements of the individual's chosen trade. Fitters would learn about the running and maintenance of engines used in aircraft or mechanical transport, or the rigging, repair and maintenance of aircraft components and airframes. On successful completion of the course, ex-apprentices were posted to a unit to exercise their trade under skilled supervision. Having followed a broadly similar pattern of training, the Fitter (Armourer) would be able to maintain all aspects of armament including rifles, machine guns, gun interrupter gear, bombs and their associated equipment. Electricians would undertake maintenance and repair of all electrical gear, other than wireless and heavy electrical permanent plant. Instruction in the trade of Instrument Maker included the maintenance and repair of instruments, cameras and bomb sights.

Whilst the war brought many changes to apprentice and other training at Halton, it also brought a brief spell of operational activity at the aerodrome. Between 11th November and 9th December 1940, 112 (RCAF) Squadron operated Lysander IIs from Halton, before transferring to Digby to become 2 Fighter Squadron, and then 402 Squadron. Later, on 15th June 1943, 529 Squadron formed from 1448 (Calibration) Flight. The latter unit, a lodger unit of 60 Group at Leighton Buzzard, used a number of Cierva autogyros on radar calibration duties, and moved to Henley-on-Thames on 19th August 1944.

It was also in 1944 than another Halton tradition was inaugurated - the adoption of a goat as the band's mascot. A short-haired Welsh mountain goat, which had been born in January 1944, arrived at Halton in June that year from the Melksham base of the Welsh Fusiliers. The name Lewis was coined from the initial letters of the words London, England, Wales, Ireland and Scotland and ACII Lewis first paraded with the band on the Jubilee Parade in May 1945. Having made many ceremonial appearances with the band, Lewis was finally retired in October 1947 to be replaced by Lewis II, born on St Patrick's Day, 17th March 1947. Lewis II was presented to the Pipe Band by Mrs Liddington, a local resident. After a period of some twenty years without a mascot, Lewis V was born on 16th April, 1980, whilst Lewis VI and Lewis VII were on parade together for the graduation of the 142nd Entry on 15th October 1986.

The war also saw the arrival at Halton of the first Polish boys for training in the Polish Technical Training School. An advance party of ten officers and 199 boys arrived in August 1943, and Polish training continued at Halton until 12th March 1948, when the Polish

Apprentice School closed. By 1945, over 18,000 apprentices had been trained at the various schools, and the 25th Anniversary of the Scheme was marked at Halton on Friday, 25th May by a parade which was reviewed by Marshal of the Royal Air Force, the Viscount Trenchard, GCB GCVO DSO DCL LLD. Trenchard was accompanied by Marshal of the Royal Air Force, Sir Charles Portal, GCB DSO MC, Chief of the Air Staff.

Post-War Consolidation

With the end of the war, it was announced in October 1945 that from the following year the apprentice scheme would expand again, with three intakes per year from May 1946, each 500-strong. During the war, the aircraft apprenticeship had been the only method of regular entry to the RAF and with the retention of National Service, the ex-apprentice became the core of regular personnel in a largely conscript Air Force. However, in a reflection of the reaction seen in the years following the First World War, the interest of the Nation in voluntary military service was low, with some entries taking in as few as 80 recruits, whilst the average was about 150. By the late 1950s, however, numbers steadily rose until more than 2,000 apprentices were in training at Halton.

Technical training occupied about half of the working time of the apprentice, which included a sound basic engineering training

Top right: **The distinguished gathering for the Silver Jubilee parade in 1945 included Marshals of the RAF, the Viscount Trenchard and Sir Charles Portal, accompanied by (from Trenchard's immediate right) Air Commodore H G White, Commandant; Air Marshal Sir Arthur S Barratt, AOC in C Training Command (2nd right); and Air Vice-Marshal K M St C C Leask, AOC 24 Group (rear).** via HAAA

Bottom: **In April 1947, General Piolet, Chief of Staff of the French Air Force, together with the Prime Minister, Mr Attlee, visited Halton to view a flying demonstration by aircraft of the RAF.** via HAAA

followed by varied specialist training depending upon his trade. About 25% of the course consisted of educational training, in such skills as mathematics, science and engineering drawing as well as English and general studies. The Halton training was recognised for the award of the Ordinary National Certificate in Mechanical or Electrical Engineering and for the award of certificates by the City and Guilds of London Institute.

The character of the apprentice was developed in a variety of ways, including the discipline of the parade ground and the use of Service hand-guns. There was, however, much more varied training. All apprentices attended and annual two-week summer camp spent under canvas, often in Wales. During the camp such activities as fieldcraft, map reading, escape and evasion exercises, physical training and swimming would be carried out. This general Service training was a key factor in the development of an individual's character, including his powers of self-reliance, initiative and leadership.

Such was the reputation of the RAF's Apprentice Scheme that the representatives of many air forces from around the world visited the RAF to see what it involved. One such visitor to Halton in March 1947 was a delegation of the Supreme Soviet of the USSR whilst the following month, General Piolet, Chief of Staff of the French Air Force, visited Halton with the Prime Minister, Mr Attlee, to view a flying demonstration by aircraft of the home Commands.

The importance of the Apprentice Scheme received the recognition of Her Majesty The Queen when No 1 School of Technical Training was honoured with the

Below: **Ansons VP533 and VM377 at Halton, 18th October 1959, to provide air experience flights for apprentices.** C F E Smedley

Opposite page: **Apprentices prepare to launch another Sedbergh glider sortie in February 1975.** via HAAA

presentation of a Colour. The presentation was made by The Queen herself on 25th July 1952, an occasion which saw 1,700 apprentices on parade. That year also saw the end of a short-lived scheme where all apprentices of the same trade were allocated to the same Wing, thus splitting each entry across the three Wings. The scheme was not welcomed and there was great rejoicing when the entries were reunited again on the same Wing. In the years following the war, Halton and its fellow schools also trained many apprentices from overseas, particularly from the countries of The Commonwealth.

As a further spur to character development, a Glider Training Flight was formed to give apprentices air experience flights and it began operations on 17th March 1945. Basic instruction was given on Dagling gliders, followed by the Kirby Cadet, with a two-seat Kranich being added in 1946. By 1948 Cadet Mk IIs had arrived and in 1950 an example of the ubiquitous Slingsby T-21B Sedbergh was obtained. This latter type was to become the mainstay of the Glider Flight until the late 1980s when use was made of the motor gliders of the resident 613 Voluntary Gliding School.

Another organisation undertaking air experience flying for the apprentices was the Station Flight. Initially, the flight operated Dominies, but in 1947 these were replaced by Anson Xs and an Anson XIX, which were also supplemented by a number of Tiger Moths. The air experience flying role also extended to the trainees at Cosford and St Athan, and to the officer cadets at Spitalgate and Kirton in Lindsey. Later, the flight was re-equipped with the Chipmunk, which became its mainstay for many years. Latterly, with the departure of the Chipmunks, the apprentice air experience role was taken over by the resident motor gliders of 613 VGS.

As well as providing for the needs of the apprentices and other trainees, the Station Flight also served Bomber Command Headquarters, at nearby High Wycombe, the HQ 24 Group whilst it was located at Halton and the HQ 60 Group at Leighton Buzzard,

which was responsible for the control and calibration of all the radar sites throughout the British Isles. A varied fleet of aircraft was available to the Flight for these duties, including in 1940 eight Magisters, a Hornet Moth and a Proctor. From January 1943 an Air Training Corps Flight was formally established to operate two Dominies and an Oxford to provide air experience flying for air cadets in camp at Halton and elsewhere. A separate Bomber Command Communications Flight was hived off from the Station Flight in the spring of 1943, but it remained located at Halton due to lack of space at Booker. This flight slowly expanded in size, to include a Hornet Moth, three Austers, five Proctors, three Oxfords and a Dakota, although the latter aircraft was based at Northolt.

Whilst over the years many trades had been rendered redundant, new trades were introduced in their place. The horizons of the apprentice had expanded greatly in the face of vastly more complex weapons systems and new scientific discoveries. Despite the astonishing rate of change of technology, which over just a few years saw jet replace piston, and the introduction of rockets, the basic concept of apprentice training continued unchanged. The aim of the RAF was not only to turn boys into experienced and qualified tradesmen, but also to turn them into men, and the moulding of character was considered of prime importance since Halton first began as an apprentice training school. Thus, the aim was still the same.

'To produce advanced tradesmen of good education and to develop in them such qualities of character - sense of responsibility, leadership, and pride of service - as will fit them for a progressive career within the Royal Air Force'.   Air Ministry, 1959.

Planning for the Future
In late 1960 a study was initiated into the RAF's youth training requirements. This was undertaken in parallel with another study into the requirements for trade specialisations and resulted in the 1964 Trade Structure, introduced in April that year. The aim of the two studies was to match the growing complexity of RAF aircraft and their systems, particularly those anticipated on the TSR-2, with groundcrew who had the ability to diagnose faults in systems which cut across the traditional trade boundaries.

Above: **HRH The Princess Margaret, presents a replacement Queen's Colour to No.1 SofTT on 6th April 1968. She is assisted by the Commandant, Air Cdre H P Connolly.** via HAAA

Above right: **Apprentices assisted with the restoration of Spitfire SL574 prior to its delivery to San Diego. The aircraft is seen here in September 1987, when the work was partially complete.** Author

The RAF's previous reliance on maintenance by repair was being superseded by a new concept of repair by replacement, with failed components often being returned to the manufacturer for repair.

As a result, the single-skill Aircraft Apprentice was replaced by a new breed, the Technician Apprentice, who trained in the four trades of airframe, propulsion, electrical and weapons. Technician Apprentices were recruited with a minimum of four GCE O-levels and, after a period of intense debate, it was decided that they would graduate in the

rank of Corporal. The new scheme was also designed to give the Technician Apprentice an Ordinary National Certificate in Engineering, and the entry numbering sequence followed the earlier Aircraft Apprentice series.

Simultaneously with the introduction of the Technician Apprentice, to meet the RAF's need for skilled craftsmen, the Craft Apprenticeship was introduced in the previous single skills, although the course length was reduced to two years and a new series of entry numbers in the 200 series was introduced. From 1959 a small number of Dental Technician Apprentices had been trained at Halton and from 1964 they were integrated with the appropriate aircraft technician course. In October 1969, a one-year mechanic apprentice course was introduced, with entry numbers in the 400 series.

In the 1970s the Princess Mary's Royal Air Force Hospital was expanded with the construction of a new surgical unit and other facilities. The Institute of Health and Community Medicine was formed and the

Institute of Dental Health and Technology was rehoused in new, purpose-built accommodation incorporating specialist teaching facilities. The Halton airfield technical training facilities were also enhanced for the first time since before the war with the construction of a new hangar to house the expanded facilities required for the introduction of training for Flight Line Mechanics.

Following the pre-war success of the Halton Aeroplane Club, further acclaim came as a result of the efforts of Flight Lieutenant, later Squadron Leader, John Potter and his band of enthusiastic supporters who formed the Halton Manpowered Aircraft Group. With the help of the Royal Aeronautical Society, the Group obtained an earlier project from Woodford and took it to Halton in September 1970. The aircraft needed to be rebuilt following damage sustained in a fire in 1969, and after a great deal of effort it was ready for flight in early 1972. Conditions were right for the Jupiter's first flight which was made at Benson on 9th February 1972, when John Potter took it aloft to become only the fifth man-powered aircraft to fly in the country. After a flying career spanning in excess of fifty flights, the Jupiter was allocated the BAPC Register number 127 and placed on display in the Foulkes-Halbard Collection, at Filching Manor, Wannock, near Eastbourne.

Other flying activities at Halton have seen the annual Air Show, which attracts large crowds and a variety of aircraft to the little grass aerodrome. At weekends the aerodrome buzzes with the activities of 613 VGS, the Halton Flying Club and the Chiltern Gliding Club of the RAF Gliding and Soaring Association. In 1981, members of the Flying Club obtained the Kittiwake Mk II, G-AWGM, for rebuilding to flying condition.

Such activities have not, however, been restricted to recreational flying. In 1987 apprentices were involved in the restoration of Spitfire SL574 which went to San Diego in exchange for a P-51 Mustang which is now displayed in the RAF Museum at Hendon. Earlier, in 1960 and 1961, apprentices had assisted with the restoration of the Cierva Autogyro (AP507) and the Me 163 Komet (191316) displayed in the Science Museum's new Aeronautical Gallery from 1963. Full-sized aircraft replicas were also built for display purposes by the RAF, including a BE-2c (6252/BAPC-41) and an Avro 504 (H1968/BAPC-42 - the aircraft serial denoting the replica's origin and year of manufacture).

Her Royal Highness The Princess Margaret visited Halton on 9th April 1968, to present a replacement Queen's Colour to No.1 School of Technical Training during the Passing Out Parade of the 108th, 206th and 309th entries. The Queen's Colour has been paraded at Royal Weddings, State Funerals and route lining for visiting Heads of State, in addition to many Service events, including a visit of Her Majesty The Queen to Halton on 18th July 1980, on the occasion of the 60th Anniversary of the Apprentice Scheme. A second replacement Queen's Colour was presented on 25th September 1990, by Air Vice-Marshal His Royal Highness The Duke of Kent, on the occasion of the graduation of the 150th Entry.

The Science Museum Me163 is dismantled for refurbishment. via HAAA

In a unique tradition, the Queen's Colour of No.1 School of Technical Training is the only Queen's Colour or Standard of the RAF to be borne by a non-commissioned Colour Bearer.

Training Airframes

No study of Halton or the Apprentice Scheme would be complete without a brief look at No 1 S of TT's voracious appetite for ground instructional airframes. Even in the days before the apprentice scheme, Halton's aerodrome was equipped with a number of training aircraft, including RE-8s, all housed in canvas-covered Bessonneaux hangars. Indeed, the Bessonneaux hangars have been a feature of Halton throughout its existence. Further airframes were located in the workshops, including examples of the SE-5 which were used for training the Australian boys. With the build-up of apprentice training, more and more airframes arrived, including

a large number of Avro 504s. In some cases the airframes used in the workshops were less than complete, the apprentices spending many hours learning about the construction, maintenance and repair of mainplane panels and control surfaces, in addition to the fuselage frames.

When they passed to the aerodrome phase of their training, the aim was for the apprentices to draw together all elements of their training to practice and gain experience of aeroplane handling. In 1924, the aerodrome housed Bristol Fighters, Sopwith Snipes and Avro 504s, examples of which were flown in the 1924 Aerial Pageant at Hendon by pilots on the staff of the school. Such practically-orientated training was a theme of the whole apprenticeship, the boys being allocated worn-out airframes to rebuild to airworthy standard. Similarly, the Fitter (Aero Engines) boys were given worn out engines to overhaul, which were subsequently sent to the Home Aircraft Depot, Henlow, for testing. In some cases, engines overhauled in the workshops were sent to

Above: **Training airframes on the airfield for the King's Birthday Parade, 3rd June 1923. Types represented include the Sopwith Snipe (E7716 and 7545), Avro 504, Bristol Fighter and DH.9A.** via Bruce Robertson

Below left: **Lancaster III LM657 was the pride of Halton's post-war fleet, having flown 58 operations with 619 Sqn. It was allocated the instructional aircraft number 5602M in September 1945.** via HAAA

Below right: **Amongst the many derelict aircraft on the airfield dump in September 1958 were remnants of Meteors and Mosquitos including (centre) Mosquito 6674M/NT422.** via MCP

Above: The Beaufighter 'Cockpit Classroom' in full cry during 1953. In this case the aircraft is fitted with three-bladed propellers which were later replaced with four-bladers.
P.H.T.Green

Below: Formerly operated by the Day Fighter Leaders' School at West Raynham, Hunter F.1 WW601 became 7538M on allocation for instructional duties at Halton in early 1958.
via MCP

the aerodrome for installation and running in the training airframes.

By 1926, work was being carried out on components from Gloster Grebes and Lynx-powered Avro 504s. Further Gloster aircraft, this time Gamecocks, became available in 1929, and Armstrong Whitworth Siskins and Westland Wapitis were eagerly anticipated by the staff. During 1930, apprentices carried out repairs to the hull of a flying boat (thought to be a Short Mussel) sent to Halton from Felixstowe, part of Coastal Area, which was to be returned to service. The skills of the new Metal Rigger apprentices were eagerly awaited by the RAF at large. By 1933 the Wapitis had arrived, together with Hawker Harts

By the outbreak of war, metal-skinned aircraft had arrived in large numbers. As early as 1938, Fairey Battles and Bristol Blenheim fighters were in use, and these were increased in number as the training machine wound up the output of mechanics to meet the desperate need for aircraft groundcrew. A wide variety of aircraft found their way to Halton, including large numbers of Spitfires, Hurricanes and even Herefords. Notable aircraft included the second prototype Manchester (L7247/2738M) and later the prototype Lincoln (PW925/6141M). The latter aircraft unfortunately caught fire during engine running training with the 54th Entry in 1949 and was destroyed.

Following the end of the war there was a plentiful supply of aircraft available for training purposes and the use of war veterans continued well into the 1950s. One of Halton's prized possessions of this era was Lancaster Mk III, LM657, formerly of 619 Squadron and a veteran of 58 operations; it was flown in to Halton in 1945 by a lady pilot of the ATA. In 1952 an Anson 1 arrived and it was hoped to equip the aircraft for use as a flying classroom.

Obtaining up-to-date training aids and equipment has always been a problem for the training organisation and at any time of national crisis the situation is made even worse. So it was at Halton in the early 1950s,

Above: **XA892/7746M was the first of three Vulcans to see service at Halton.** Author

Below: **Sea Vixen 8142M/XJ560 was delivered to Halton in the early 1970s.** Author

with the Korean conflict delaying the arrival of more modern, jet-powered aircraft. However, by 1953, Meteor 3s and Vampire 3s had started to trickle in to allow the training to be made more appropriate to the needs of the front-line squadrons, although the instructional staffs were still disappointed at the lack of other types such as the Hastings, Canberra and the later marks of Meteor. Venoms put in an appearance by 1954 and a Lincoln was in use for bombing-up and engine-running training. Some surprise arrivals in 1955 included Neville Duke's record breaking Hunter (WB188/7154M), the Hawker P1052 (VX272/7174M) and the Supermarine 510 (VV106/7175M). It was not until 1956 that Meteor 8s arrived in any quantity, together with a handful of Swifts. The brunt of Halton's training until the mid-1950s was therefore borne by the wartime types, especially the Mosquito which was used in some numbers until the ravages of continuous use by the apprentices and the weather saw them scrapped in about 1958.

One unique survivor of the wartime era was the Beaufighter, another type to equip Halton in some numbers. In an ingenious concept, one Beaufighter had its rear fuselage replaced by a wooden hut to form the famous 'Cockpit Classroom'. The aircraft's various engine controls and indicators were run from the cramped cockpit into the wooden hut to allow the instructor to give practical tuition in engine starting and running to a whole class simultaneously, rather than to just one student at a time which was the only possible solution using the aircraft cockpit. The Cockpit Classroom survived for many years, until it was dismantled and is now under restoration to flying condition in Bedfordshire. Subsequent research has

shown that the aircraft was Beaufighter IF X7688, formerly of 143 and 29 Squadrons, which was allocated the instructional aircraft number 3858M in June 1943 and is now registered G-DINT.

With the installation of Swifts in Workshops, Airframe Fitter Flt was able to pension off some if its remaining wartime training aids, including a Lancaster cockpit section and a Spitfire fuselage. The long-awaited Canberras began to arrive in 1957, together with the first of what was to become a key training aircraft for two decades or more, the Hunter. With the arrival of large numbers of Hunter 4s, the venerable Meteor was pensioned off in 1963.

The first of two Comets to see service at Halton, Mk 2X prototype G-ALYT (7610M), was flown in by John Cunningham during May 1959, having seen service as a development airframe for the installation of the Avon engine. This aircraft was scrapped in 1967, along with a few Javelins which had arrived in 1961, to be replaced by Comet C2 XK716 (7958M), flown in from Lyneham the same year. Halton's small grass airfield was no deterrent to the aerial delivery of large, high performance jet aircraft. The first of three Vulcans (XA892/7746M) was flown in on 22nd June, 1962, by Squadron Leader D S Bell, one of Farnborough's test pilots. A second Vulcan (XA898/7856M) followed in 1964, and XH479 (7974M) arrived in 1967. Other aerial deliveries have included Argosies and Canberras.

In recent years Halton has become synonymous with the Jet Provost, which began to arrive for mechanic training in 1969. Further aircraft were delivered from 1971, together with Gnats and Sea Hawks, when Hawker Siddeley started to remove a large number of Hunters for sale overseas. Not all of Halton's aircraft were housed on the airfield, because large numbers were used in the New Workshops and, to a lesser extent, in the Old Workshops. The aircraft in workshops were predominantly the smaller types, especially the Hunter, Jet Provost and Gnat, although English Electric P1B XG329/8050M

Above: **Apprentice Engineering Technicians practice aircraft maintenance activities on a Jaguar.** via HAAA

was a prized possession in New Workshops following its arrival in 1970.

With 1971 there came an influx of Sea Vixens from the Royal Navy, presenting the instructional staff with quite a challenge to integrate them successfully into the training syllabus. In comparison with previous training aircraft the Sea Vixen was complicated, having four hydraulic systems, an arrester hook, an underwater ejection system and dive brakes, all potential traps for the unwary. However, the task was completed successfully and from 1972 the Sea Vixens helped replace the Hunters sold to Hawker Siddeley. The year 1971 also saw the scrapping of two of the Vulcans (XA892 and XA898) and the arrival of an Argosy, whilst the Canberras and Piston Provosts began to leave the following year.

Above: **With the advent of the Harrier GR.5 and GR.7, the elderly GR.3s were relegated to instructional use. This particular former 4 Squadron example, coded 'B' on the fin, is probably 9074M (ex-XV738).** Author

Below: **With engineering training due to cease at Halton, the training airframes are slowly being removed from the workshops. Jet Provost XM411/8434M is seen awaiting disposal in September 1992.** Author

Most recently, the bulk of the training fleet has comprised Gnats and Jet Provosts. However, as the Tornado entered front-line service, a number of Jaguars were released to give the training fleet a much needed boost in technology. Moreover, Adour engines from the Jaguars provided up-to-date modular engines as training aids for the propulsion technicians. Further enhancement of the training fleet came when the first of a number of Harrier GR.3s, were flown in for use in the New Workshops.

A Time of Change

Unfortunately for the aspiring fault diagnosticians, the Government's cancellation of the TSR-2 undermined the planned employment of the new-style multi-skilled Aircraft Technician. Initially they were put to work on the RAF's current fleet where they were unable to demonstrate their multi-trade flair. As a result of this factor, together with the introduction of the one-year Direct Entry Technician scheme, and cessation of the Craft Apprenticeship in the early 1970s, there grew a concern that a remedy was needed to restore the shortcomings of the Technician Apprenticeship. After further study, it was decided to introduce the three-year dual-trade Aircraft Engineering Technician Apprentice specialising in just two trades, airframe and propulsion.

By the mid-1980s, however, difficulties were being experienced in recruiting sufficient apprentices to meet the RAF's needs. Attempts to increase the frequency of entries to three per year were thwarted by the inevitable attachment to the academic year and school examinations. The Apprentice Scheme was seen as having lost its appeal to the youth of the day, many of whom sought technical qualifications by alternative means following their secondary education, or who opted for the more attractive short-term financial rewards of the RAF's Direct Entry Technician scheme. Moreover, the forecast movement of demographic trends saw increasing difficulty in achieving apprentice recruiting targets in future years.

New studies into the RAF's need for high grade tradesmen into the next century began in 1989 under the Aircraft Engineering Trades Review, the results of which were implemented in April 1991. The AETR introduced a 'single gate, dual stream' method of entry to the flagship aircraft engineering trades, in which all tradesmen are trained initially as mechanics. After a period of up to two years productive service, the technician stream mechanics and later some of the mechanic stream tradesmen will be selected for Further Training to become technicians. After more productive service, particularly able technicians will be selected for Advanced Further Training, leading to the award of a BTEC Higher Certificate.

It would, however, be easy to despair at the passing of the Apprentice Scheme, but the RAF's need for high grade tradesmen is now greater than ever before. The technology for which the Technician Apprentice was conceived in 1964 is now in service in aircraft like the Harrier GR.7 and the Tornado. On the horizon is the Eurofighter 2000, with ever-more complex systems and technology. Superimposed on the need for these skills has been the growing pressure on the RAF for greater cost-effectiveness and the impact of the Government's Options for Change requirements. The latter pressures will see the end of engineering training at Halton as the size of the RAF's training machine is trimmed down. However, following early doubts that it might close, Halton will remain open as the centre for basic recruit and administrative training. During 1993 and 1994, all aircraft engineer training, together with the title of No 1 School of Technical Training, will move to Cosford.

A measure of the Halton Tradition may be gained from this scene as many hundreds of Old Haltonians re-enact the march back to Wings during the September 1992 reunion of the Halton Aircraft Apprentices Association.
Author

The Halton Tradition

As old as the RAF itself, Halton has inspired a strong and creative tradition of many facets which refuses to be bound by rank, time or service. It is difficult to define that tradition, which is in part the sense of belonging to a club or society. In part, it is the realisation that the education given by Halton was complete. In part, it is the realisation that Halton was a firm but tolerant guardian during that difficult transition from youth to adult. In most ex-Haltonians there is gratitude: there is pleasure: there is pride. The Entry spirit slowly expands to become the Halton Tradition as individuals recognise that each is a member of a continuing society, the common basis of which is the Halton Apprenticeship.

Trenchard's Legacy

So what did Trenchard achieve when he conceived the Apprentice Scheme? He laid the foundation for a core of highly skilled tradesmen which, in 1939, formed the engineering backbone of the RAF on which the expansion was built. Over 20% of Halton apprentices went on to be commissioned, with over half reaching Squadron Leader rank or higher and many reaching Air rank. As for success, Sir Frank Whittle was an apprentice and Sergeant Thomas Gray, one of seven brothers, four of whom were Halton apprentices, was awarded the Victoria Cross. Halton alone has produced some 35,000 apprentices who, over the years, have established an ethos and an *esprit de corps* which is revered around the world.

With the graduation of Halton's 155th Entry in June 1993, followed by Cosford's entry in October, the RAF Apprenticeship Scheme ended. Ex-apprentices have served the Nation well and have forged a reputation for excellence which extends throughout the world. The Royal Air Force can look back on Halton and Trenchard's Brats with well-founded pride.

HALTON
THE 1920s

Top right: **East Camp, Halton Park, in the summer of 1915. The tents have been replaced by wooden huts; the building on the right is officers' accommodation.**
via HAAA

Right: **Leyland Lorries dominated the MT fleet at Halton when this photograph was taken on 22nd January 1920.**
RAF Museum P016897 via HAAA

Below: **With its sign proclaiming Halton Camp East, the MT yard stands by the side of the public road which bisects the station. Today the MT yard occupies the same location.** RAF Museum P016898 via HAAA

Right: **Some of the first RAF maintenance personnel mounting the guard at Halton in 1918.** via HAAA

Below: **Some of the first trainees receive instruction in the newly built workshops at Halton. The trainees come from both the RFC and the Australian Flying Corps, whilst the aircraft are S.E.5 A4849 and R.E.8 A4166.** via Bruce Robertson

Halton: The 1920s

Photographs on this page, from the top:

This final page of pre-Apprentice wooden-hut era illustrations begins with the interior of one of Halton's huts, in this case the quarters of an officer. via HAAA

The first RAF trained draft of technical personnel prepares to leave Halton on 11th September 1920. via HAAA

The huts of North Camp nestle in a clearing in the woods whilst the airfield can be seen in the distance with some six Bessonneaux hangars visible. via HAAA

Photographs on the opposite page, from the top, left to right:

A later view of North Camp, showing the two Type F hangars on the airfield. Reputedly, these came from France to Halton. via HAAA

Bulback Barracks when nearly complete in 1922. Builders' debris and huts occupy what was to become the parade ground. Beyond the barracks are the massive workshops and further hutted camp areas. via HAAA

The Maitland barracks area, seen here shortly after completion, was at first known as Chiltern Barracks. In the foreground can be seen four of the eight barrack blocks, the Institute, the Mess Hall, the Headquarters; and through the trees, the Guardroom. Beyond the parade ground lie more huts and the three barrack blocks of Shepherd Barracks have yet to be built. via HAAA

Chiltern and Bulback Barracks complete in 1925; quarters for married airmen have been built and work is underway on the hospital to the left of the picture. via HAAA

Maitland, Henderson and Groves Barracks, married quarters and the hospital. The Shepherd and Paine Barracks were to come later. via HAAA

The Guardroom at the entrance to Bulback Barracks, seen here in 1923, shortly after completion. via HAAA

THE NORTH CAMP. HALTON. R.A.F.

R.A.F. BARRACKS. AT. HALTON. 1922

THE NEW BARRACKS. R.A.F. HALTON

GENERAL VIEW OF HALTON CAMP 1925

BULBACK BARRACKS R.A.F HALTON

ENTRANCE TO BULBACK BARRACKS. HALTON. R.A.F.

Halton: The 1920s

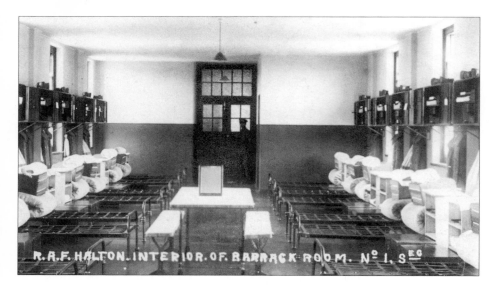

R.A.F. HALTON. INTERIOR OF BARRACK ROOM. No 1. SEC

Left: The somewhat crowded living conditions of apprentices can be seen in this 1923 view of a barrack room on No.1 Section (later No.1 Wing). via HAAA

Centre left: The HQ of No.4 Wing, on the Maitland Barracks area. A captured German field gun adorns the HQ entrance, one of a number of such trophies at one time displayed at Halton. The stark surroundings are now relieved by a few trees. via HAAA

Bottom left: A barrack room on No.4 Wing, in about 1923, showing a slightly different method of bed preparation to that seen on No.1 Section (Wing). via HAAA

Bottom right: The upper floor of the dining hall on No.4 Wing, Maitland Barracks, in the late 1920s. Whilst sparsely equipped, the dining hall could feed hundreds of hungry apprentices in a very short time. via HAAA

GUARD ROOM

Opposite page, centre left: **The Guardroom at the entrance to Chiltern (later Maitland) Barracks. To the left can be seen the MT yard whilst the roof of the Astra Cinema can be seen to the right.** via HAAA

This page, top left: **The spiritual welfare of the apprentices was cared for by a number of Churches, including the Church of England which was located in part of the workshops. In this view, taken in 1929, the lectern presented by members of the 1st Entry, can be clearly seen.** via HAAA

Top right: **In addition to the Churches themselves, the Church Clubs also aided spiritual welfare, as seen in this view of the Roman Catholic Church Club.** via HAAA

Right: **Halton's cinema, seen here in the 1920s, has been a key feature of the station's recreational facilities until today.** via HAAA

Halton: The 1920s

Top left: **The newly completed Institute at No.4 Wing, Maitland Barracks.** via HAAA

Top right: **Billiards was the dominant recreation on the upper floor of the No.4 Wing Institute.** via HAAA

Centre: **The closely packed seating in the No.4 Wing Institute gives an idea of the numbers that could be accommodated.** via HAAA

Left: **Whilst the design and construction of the No.1 Wing Institute shows great similarity with that of No.4 Wing, the furniture provides an interesting contrast. In this case, the word NAAFI is engraved in the top rail of the wooden seat backs.** via HAAA

Right: **Seen on parade for Church on 18th September 1921, Halton had a band and two goat mascots even before the arrival of the apprentices.** via HAAA

Below: **Armistice Day on 11th November always saw a major parade at Halton. Before the large parade grounds were built, most parades were held on the grass in front of the Workshops building.** via HAAA

Above: **The schools building was at first intended to be a record office. Extended after this view was taken in 1922, the schools building is now named Kermode Hall.** via HAAA

Below: **The Passing Out Parade of an unknown entry in the 1920s.** via HAAA

Above: **An inspection by HRH The Duke of York in December 1922 would have been one of the first major parades on the new Bulback Barracks parade ground. The large building in the background is the No.2 Wing dining hall.** via HAAA

Right: **Once again looking towards No.2 Wing (later Groves Barracks), the Armistice Day Commemoration on 11th November 1926, saw large numbers of apprentices on parade.** via HAAA

Below: **Led by an officer, the apprentices of No.4 Section (later Wing) depart from the Workshops area following a Church parade.** via HAAA

Top: **Bulback Barracks' hallowed parade ground serves as a meeting place for apprentices and their parents at the first Parents Day, held on 26th July 1924.** via HAAA

Above: **No.3 Section, led by its band, marches up to Main Point on its way to Workshops.** via HAAA

Above: **Drum Major Hughes, of Halton's 1st Entry in January 1922 (the 5th Entry of the Apprentice Scheme) photographed in 1923. He attained the rank of Flight Lieutenant before retiring in 1946.** via HAAA

Above: **The No.2 Section band practices in 1924. Just visible on the hats of the bands-men are a variety of coloured hatbands and the numeral '2' attached above the hat badge to denote No.2 Section.** via HAAA

Above right: **Apprentices on the march - a traditional scene at Halton throughout its life. In this case, the apprentices comprise No.2 Section (later Wing) photographed on 26th October 1922.** via HAAA

Below: **Bands have been one of Halton's key features. Here, the No.1 Section Band is seen in the early 1920s.** via HAAA

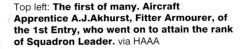

Top left: **The first of many. Aircraft Apprentice A.J.Akhurst, Fitter Armourer, of the 1st Entry, who went on to attain the rank of Squadron Leader.** via HAAA

Top right: **A scene in Workshops in 1922 with a group of Aircraft Apprentices learning the intricacies of rigging.** via HAAA

Centre left: **Carpenter Riggers of the 6th Entry, in front of an example of their handiwork to the rear of Workshops.** via HAAA

Bottom left: **Carpenter riggers of the 10th or 11th Entry undergo basic carpentry training in July 1925.** via HAAA

Photographs on the opposite page:

Top left: **In this 1922 scene in Workshops a group of apprentices make use of a Bristol Fighter, probably M61 (though possibly M161).** via HAAA

Top right: **The scene to the rear of workshops during a break in lessons, thought to have been taken in 1922.** via HAAA

Bottom: **Carpenter Riggers undertake advanced training in 1922.** via HAAA

Top left: **The first two permanent hangars erected on Halton's aerodrome. The hangars are of the Type F design, and are locally reputed to have been brought from France, although this has not been substantiated.** via HAAA

Centre left: **The 6th Entry Airframe Riggers Course photographed during its aerodrome training.** via HAAA

Bottom: **The King's Birthday parade in 1924. A variety of aircraft can be seen including the D.H.9A (E9891), Bristol Fighter (F4581), Avro 504 and Sopwith Snipe.** via HAAA

Photograph on opposite page, bottom left:

Apprentices gain experience of the practical problems of handling parachutes on the ground. via HAAA

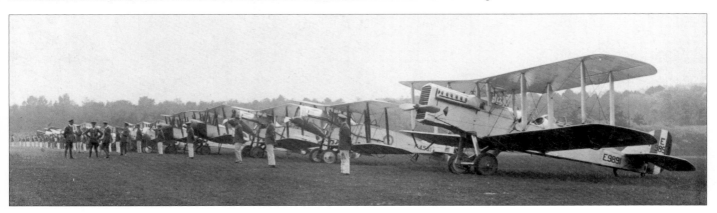

R.A.F. HALTON. A.A.S. AERODROME. COURSE. 25-6-24.

Above: **Aircraft apprentices clearly enjoying their aerodrome course in June 1924.** via HAAA

Bottom right: **A Sopwith Snipe, carrying the partially obstructed serial number 'INSTR 16?M' is here filling a vital role training the RAF's future technicians.** P H T Green

R.A.F. HALTON. A.A.S. IN TRAINING.

Top left: **Physical training was a vital element of the Halton regime. Here the boys of No.2 Section are being put through their paces.** via HAAA

Top right: **Halton's programme of physical training was intended not only to improve physical fitness, but also to develop the individual's character and team spirit. Such qualities are seen here, being demonstrated by the B Squadron, No.2 Section, PT Team, in 1925.** via HAAA

Centre left: **Boxing was a strongly supported sport at Halton for many years. The victorious Halton team is seen here in 1925, following the defeat of Cranwell in the Barton Challenge Cup competition.** via HAAA

Bottom left: **The workshops complex also housed a large swimming pool, seen here in 1925.** via HAAA

Photographs on the opposite page:

Top: **The vast size of the Workshops complex gave Halton the opportunity to develop an indoor boxing stadium, which is seen here prepared for a competition in 1926 under the auspices of the Imperial Services Boxing Association.** via HAAA

Bottom: **A boxing competition underway in 1927. The audience of apprentices seems to be enjoying the bout in progress.** via HAAA

Halton: The 1920s

Top left: **The simple but effective construction of the HAC-1's wings is seen here before the mainplane panel was covered in fabric.** via HAAA

Above left: **The HAC-1 'Mayfly' seen soon after its completion and in its initial biplane configuration.** via HAAA

Left: **The HAC-1 'Mayfly' under construction following trial installation of its Bristol Cherub engine.** via HAAA

Top right: **An artist's impression of the HAC-3 'Meteor' which was almost complete before the project was abandoned.** via HAAA

Above: **The President's Cup, won for the Halton Aero Club by Flight Lieutenant le Poer Trench at Hamble on 15th May 1927.** via HAAA

HALTON
THE 1930s

Above left: **Halton's airfield saw a number of visiting aircraft, including this impressive line-up of Siskin IIIAs from 41 Squadron, which must have taken place in, or before 1931.** via HAAA

Left: **Local photographers did a roaring trade taking photographs of room-mates in front of their barrack block. In front of Block No.2, Maitland Barracks, are the members of Room 1 on the ground floor.** via HAAA

Bottom left: **Lord Trenchard inspected the Passing Out parade of the 18th Entry at Halton on 25th July 1933. Here, Lord Trenchard is inspecting the work of Aircraft Apprentice A J Mason, Fitter (Aero Engine), winner of the Lord Wakefield Scholarship and the Elliot Memorial Prize.** via HAAA

Below: **The passing out parade of the 21st Entry, in December 1932. This parade was filmed for Movietone News.** via HAAA

Left: Members of the 34th Entry, C Squadron, No.4 Wing, enjoy themselves on the aerodrome course in 1939. via HAAA

Centre left: No.4 Wing's athletics team won the junior trophy in the 1937 Barrington-Kennett Trophy competition. via HAAA

Centre right: The pipes and drums from No.3 Wing in 1938. Members of the band came from the 33rd and 34th Entries which, towards the end of their course, were split half and half between 3 and 4 Wings. via HAAA

Above: **Members of the 34th Entry during the aerodrome course in August 1936.**
via HAAA

Above: **Members of the 36th Entry, No.1 Wing, pause for the photographer whilst in Workshops in 1938.** via HAAA

Right: **The No.4 Wing Drums in December 1938, pictured with the Wing CO, Wing Commander Swann.** via HAAA

Photographs on opposite page, bottom row:

Left: **His Majesty King George VI tours the New Workshops on 14th April 1939, where members of the 37th Entry were undertaking preliminary rigging training.** via HAAA

Right: **During his visit to Halton in April 1939, The King was given the opportunity to inspect the instructional aircraft at the aerodrome.** via HAAA

Halton: The 1930s

Left: **Expansion of the RAF saw the arrival at Halton of several monoplane aircraft. A Battle and a Blenheim (probably K7040/1042M) are seen here at Parents' Day, 1938.** via Bruce Robertson

Centre: **Blenheim K7040 (1042M) and K7060 (1043M), ex-114 and 139 Squadrons respectively, seen at Halton in 1939.** via Bruce Robertson

Bottom left: **Bulldogs, including 954M (K2135), being prepared for engine ground running in 1938.** via Bruce Robertson

Bottom right: **Hart 999M (K4327) and Bulldog 953M (K2213), part of Halton's training fleet in 1938.** via Chris Ashworth

Above: **Blenheim 1043M/K7060, formerly of 139 Sqn, is positioned on the grass and prepared for engine running in January 1939.** via HAAA

Below: **The point of ignition as the engine fires.** via HAAA

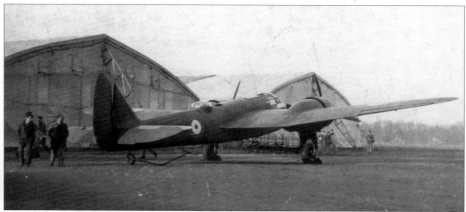

Above: **An unidentified Blenheim is positioned on the tarmac in front of the main hangars prior to engine running training in January 1939. A pair of Bessonneaux hangars stand on the edge of the airfield. The three photographs on this page have been reproduced from reverse printed paper negatives.** via HAAA

HALTON
1936 SITE PLAN

The New Workshops area, Burnett
Gymnasium, Paine and Shepherd Barracks,
which were completed by 1939, have been
added to aid reference.

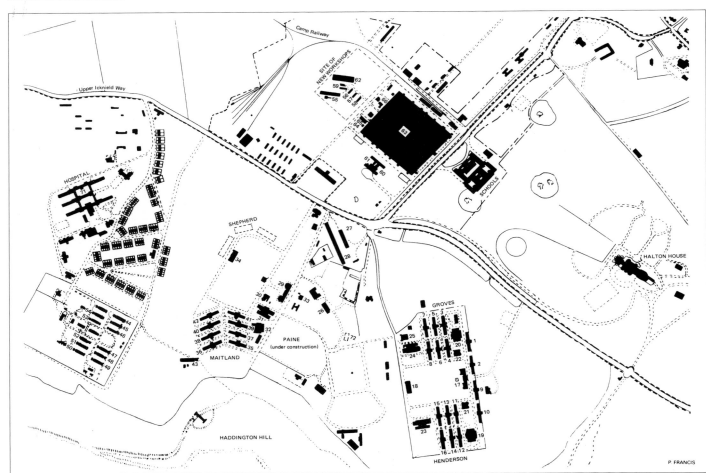

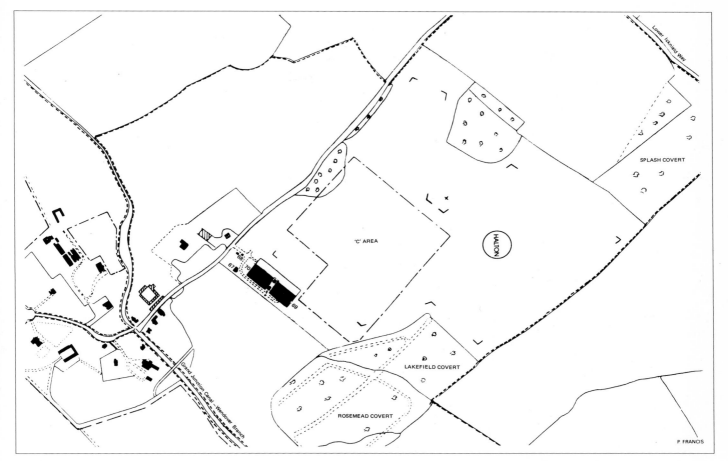

HALTON – Key to site plans

1-8	Groves Barrack blocks
9-16	Henderson Barrack blocks
17	Special block including Master Tailor's and Barber's Shops and Medical section
18	Drill shed
19-20	Institute
21	Sergeants' Mess (Henderson)
22	Sergeants' Mess (Groves)
23	Dining room and cookhouse
24	Dining room and cookhouse
25	Guardhouse (Henderson and Groves)
26	Cinema
27	Mechanical Transport yard
28	MT shed
29	Special block including armoury and shoemaker's shop.
30	Sergeants' Mess
31	Dining room (Maitland)
32	Institute
33	Heating station
34	Drill shed
35-42	Barrack block (Maitland)
43	Gymnasium
44-48	Hospital infectious diseases
49	Ward and special treatment
50-54	Hospital infectious diseases
55-59	Lecture rooms
60-61	Offices, HQ
62	Aircraft apprentice school
63	Workshops, church and gym
64-65	Engine test house
66	Engine test house
67	Accommodation (aerodrome personnel)
68	Bulk petrol store
69	Flight shed including NAAFI, bar etc.
70	Flight shed No.1 including clothing store
71	Hospital (Princess Mary)
72	Burnett Gymnasium

Reproduced with the kind permission of the Airfield Research Group. These are modified versions of drawings that appeared in their journal 'Airfield Review', No.62, April 1993 issue.

HALTON
THE 1940s

Right: **The greatcoats and chinstraps indicate a cold and windy day as a flight of apprentices practices drill in readiness for its Passing Out parade.** via HAAA

Below: **The 'Parashots' name was coined to describe a force of about 70 apprentices, mainly from the 40th Entry, formed in 1940, shortly after Dunkirk. Selection was made for strength, fitness and marksmanship. They guarded the vulnerable areas such as armouries and aerodrome.** via HAAA

Right: **The Burnett Gymnasium was opened by HRH King George VI in 1939, and found ready use for the awards ceremony and address by the Reviewing Officer following Passing Out parades.** via HAAA

Bottom right: **His Royal Highness the King visited Halton again in 1941, where he is seen inspecting the kitchen staff.** via HAAA

Below: **During his 1941 visit to Halton, the King inspects apprentices working on a gun turret.** via HAAA

Bottom: **On 27th March 1947, a delegation from the Supreme Soviet of the USSR visited Halton to investigate the Apprentice Scheme.** via HAAA

Left: **The 25th Anniversary of the Apprentice Scheme was marked at Halton on 25th May 1945, by a parade made up from the 46th, 47th, 48th, 49th and 50th Entries, supported by Polish apprentices and the Apprentice Bands. The Viscount Trenchard returns the General Salute from Sergeant Aircraft Apprentice Meadows of the 46th Entry, which graduated that day. Tragically, SAA Meadows was killed in a Lancaster crash at Hullavington shortly after graduation.** via HAAA

Photographs on the opposite page:

Top left and right: **Two contrasting views of Room 1, Block 15 in 1946. The ordered and polished scene at Christmas 1946 is quite different to a Sunday morning scene of the same year.** Chris Ashworth

Bottom: **Halton's barrack areas seen from 'Pimple Point' in the late 1940s. The barracks are named (anti-clockwise from top left) Maitland, Paine, Henderson, Groves and Shepherd, with the Princess Mary's RAF Hospital in the far centre.** Chris Ashworth

MRAF The Viscount Trenchard inspects No.1 Flight of C Squadron, commanded by Sergeant Aircraft Apprentices Ainsworth and Lithgow respectively, on the occasion of the 25th Anniversary. Group Captain Joe Ainsworth is now the archivist of the Halton Aircraft Apprentices Association, whilst the apprentice on the extreme right is Chaz Bowyer, the aviation author. via HAAA

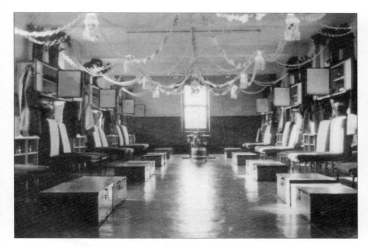

Above: **This 1940s view shows apprentices in the Schools engine performance laboratory, making use of a 9hp Ruston-Hornsby single-cylinder engine. The engine was in use until 1993.** via HAAA

Below left: **Apprentices receive instruction in the Schools building, now named** **Kermode Hall, in the latter years of the Second World War.** via HAAA

Below right: **Members of the 49th Entry receive instruction in stripping and overhaul of British Hercules engines during 1945 under the watchful eye of their instructor, Mr Cameron.** Chris Ashworth

Above: **The Pipe Band's mascot, Lewis I, seen here wearing the rank of Sergeant.** Chris Ashworth

Top: **With aircraft clustered in small groups, and barrier fences positioned to prevent accidents with rotating propellers, apprentices practice engine running in the late 1940s. The Beaufighter X is NE823/ 5757M.** via HAAA

Above: **NE823/5757M (in this case painted on the rear fuselage as M5757) was allocated for instructional duties in December 1945.** via HAAA

Above right: **Another Beaufighter of Halton's extensive fleet, unfortunately with its identity obscured.** Paddy Porter collection

Right: **A group of apprentices prepare to run-up Spitfire IX MK788/5685M.** via HAAA

Halton: The 1940s

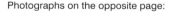

Photographs on the opposite page:

Top: **This Lancaster fuselage is likely to have been the largest aircraft to have seen use in New Workshops.** via HAAA

Bottom left: **A typical feature of Halton's workshops has been the systems 'rigs' where components are mounted on benches to simulate aircraft systems. Here hydraulic and pneumatic systems rigs are in use. In the background, the fuselage frame comes from Mosquito Mk.II W4098/4107M.** via HAAA

Bottom right: **A variety of fuel tanks were used to train apprentices. Visible in the**

picture are Typhoon R7623/3519M and Mosquito PF572/6237M. via HAAA

Photographs on this page:

Top left: **Members of the 52nd Entry study pneumatic systems amidst an exciting variety of training aircraft. These include Spitfire Vc EE600/4187M, Tempest V JN768 /4887M, together with further Typhoons, a Mosquito and some Meteors. It seems that all aircraft have been repainted in a uniform silver colour. The fuselage roundels are out-lined in another unknown colour.** via HAAA

Top right: **Apprentice engine fitters learn the basic principles of engine construction in 1946.** via HAAA

Right, second down: **Apprentices receive instruction on bombsights in Old Workshops.** via HAAA

Right, third down: **Apprentice armourers are receiving instruction about machine gun servicing.** via HAAA

Centre left: **Spitfire fuselages provide practice in metal repairs. Three Hurricane airframes are in use to train apprentices in the techniques of aero carpentry.** via HAAA

Above: **The hydraulic system from a Bristol Blenheim is seen here mounted on a test rig to allow easy demonstration of the system's operation.** via HAAA

Right: **A Manchester forms the basis for weapon loading instruction.** via HAAA

Photographs on the opposite page:

Top left: **A party of apprentices prepares to board an Anson for an air experience flight in the late 1940s.** Chris Ashworth

Top right: **Apprentices of the 58th Entry carry out basic workshops training in the New Workshops in March 1948.** via HAAA

Bottom: **Apprentice engine fitters pause from stripping Merlin engines in this 1946 Workshops scene.** via HAAA

Halton: The 1940s

HALTON
THE 1950s

Right: **Air Marshal Sir Hugh P Lloyd, AOC-in-C Bomber Command, returns the General Salute from the welcoming Guard of Honour in front of the Station Headquarters (since demolished) on his arrival for the Passing Out parade of the 56th Entry on 23rd May 1950.** via HAAA

Right: **Members of the 80th Entry celebrate graduation in traditional style, at the end of their Passing Out parade in 1958.** via HAAA

Below: **Lord Trenchard presents a prize at the awards ceremony in the Burnett Gymnasium for the 57th Entry, which passed out on 4th August 1950.** via HAAA

Top: **A bleak outlook from the Maitland parade ground at the march-past of the graduating entry, thought to be the 67th, in January 1954. Shepherd Barracks is in the background.** via HAAA

Above: **On 19th December 1956, the Minister of State for Air, the Rt Hon Nigel Birch, inspects graduating apprentices of the 76th Entry.** via HAAA

Right: **Graduating apprentices, thought to be the 77th Entry, celebrate in front of the Burnett Gymnasium in 1957.** via HAAA

Halton: The 1950s

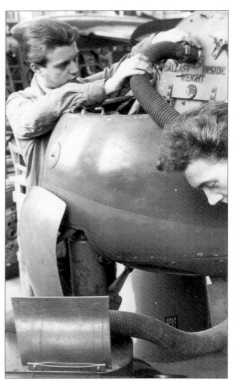

Photographs on the opposite page:

Top left: **Gun turrets, depth charges and bombs were all taught to members of the 69th Entry, Class 1, as annotated on the notice board to the right of the picture. The 69th Entry arrived at Halton in August 1951.** via HAAA

Top right: **A Hornet F.1, thought to be PX210/ 6149M, seen in the New Workshops.** Paddy Porter Collection

Bottom left: **A study of the development of aero engines was an important aspect of training apprentices destined to be engine fitters.** via HAAA

Bottom right: **A pair of apprentices conduct cabin pressurisation tests on a Venom training aircraft.** via HAAA

Photographs on this page:

Top: **A typical scene in the New Workshops in the 1950s, when the training fleet was dominated by Vampires and Meteors.** via HAAA

Right: **Apprentice instrument fitters learn about the intricacies of the automatic pilot.** via HAAA

Halton: The 1950s

Above: **Halton's Military Band, probably photographed in 1955.**
via HAAA

Below: **Anson C.19 VM377 at Halton on 18th October 1959, to carry out air experience flights. Note in the background the Station Flight and Flying Control building, which was demolished in the mid-1980s.**
C F E Smedley

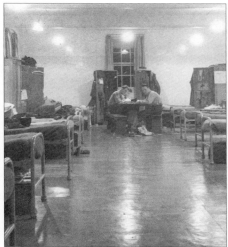

Top left: **A 1958 barrack room scene shows members of the 83rd, 85th and 86th Entries discussing their hobbies in the evening. Few will forget the daily task of polishing the 'centre deck' with a bumper, which can be seen just in front of the table.** C F E Smedley

Left: **Unforgettable barrack room scenes include the sight of the Lee-Enfield .303 No.1 Mk.4s, neatly racked at the end of each room to be readily available for rifle drill.** C F E Smedley

Top right: **An evocative view of Halton House in 1959.** C F E Smedley

Above right: **The Chipmunk dominated Halton's air experience fleet for many years. WK551 and WB552 seen here, were photographed on 20th September 1958.** MCP

Top: **Still showing signs of its former use by 100 Squadron, Canberra B.2 WF907/7386M was one of the first Canberras to arrive at Halton in early 1957.** Author's collection

Centre left: **Valetta C.2 VL276 seen at a Halton Open Day in 1958.** C F E Smedley

Bottom left: **Meteors were the predominant training type at the airfield during the 1950s. WA963/7321M wears the markings of former operator, APS Acklington. Behind are a number of Mosquitos and a Balliol.** via HAAA

Photographs on the opposite page:

Top left: **Anson C.20 VS600/7016M out to grass at Halton.** MAP

Top right: **Swift F.2 WK218/7299M at the Halton Open Day in 1958. The structure in left background was a mobile shelter which was wheeled over aircraft to allow instruction to continue in the rain.** C F E Smedley

Centre left: **Mosquito B.35 PF484/6595M starting to look a little neglected near No.4 Hangar in the late 1950s.** MAP

Centre right: **Mosquito NF.30 6659M with its previous serial NT568 just visible on the rear fuselage, became a training airframe in 1949.** via Author

Bottom: **Meteor F.3 EE397/7168M succumbs on 20th September, 1958.** MCP

Halton: The 1950s

Top left: **Also on static display at the 1958 Halton Open Day was the 4th prototype Javelin, WT830.** C F E Smedley

Top right: **Shirley the Spitfire LF.XVIe RW386 (wrongly painted as RF114) at Halton on 19th September 1959. The engine had been removed, the exhausts mounted on blocks of wood and the propeller was held on solely by a 6 inch woodscrew.** C F E Smedley

Above: **Also on view at Halton on 15th June 1959 was XD158, the Javelin FAW.2 prototype.** C F E Smedley

Left: **Comet 2X G-ALYT (allocated 7610M) at Halton on 15th June 1959.**
C F E Smedley

HALTON
THE 1960s

Shepherd, Maitland and Paine Barracks, together with Old and New Workshops, are visible in this view of Halton taken in about 1960. Henderson and Groves Barracks, Kermode Hall and the airfield are out of view to the right of the picture. Bruce Robertson

Halton: The 1960s

Top left: **A scene from the 1960s with the band leading a Guard of Honour towards Main Point.** via HAAA

Top right: **Prizewinners from the 104th Entry, seen in the Burnett Gymnasium on 6th April 1966.** via HAAA

Centre left: **HRH The Princess Alexandra inspects metalwork repairs during her tour of workshops after reviewing the graduation of the 100th Entry on 16th December 1964.** via HAAA

Bottom left: **Air Marshal Sir Edward Chilton, KBE CB, the AOC-in-C Coastal Command, reviews the 87th Entry at its graduation parade on 27th July 1960.** via HAAA

Left: **HRH The Princess Margaret is conducted around the Hunters in New Workshops by Gp Capt C V G Usher following the presentation of a replacement Queen's Colour to No.1 SofTT on 6th April 1968.** via HAAA

Opposite page: **The Halton Brass Band and Pipe Band form up at Holborn Viaduct during participation in the 1965 Lord Mayor's Parade. Such activity was a common feature of apprentice life.** via HAAA

Halton: The 1960s

Left: **Apprentice engine fitters of the 92nd Entry (May 1959 to April 1962) receive instruction on a cut-away Bristol Centaurus engine.** via HAAA

Below: **The early 1960s saw the Javelin in use at the airfield for engine running and other training. In the foreground an ejection seat is being installed.** via HAAA

XA551

Above: **The piston-powered Provost was in many ways an ideal platform for training engine starting procedures. In this scene from the late 1960s an apprentice is shown the pre-start safety checks by Chief Technician 'Lofty' Crone.** via HAAA

Above right: **Seen during its restoration at Halton on 25th July 1960, Me 163-B1 Komet 191316 rests in workshops prior to the start of work.** C F E Smedley

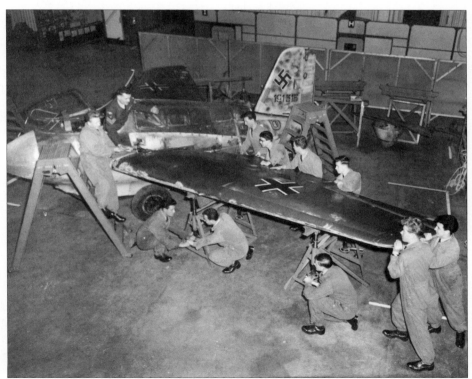

Right: **In addition to the value of the task to the Science Museum, restoration of the Museum's Komet also provided the apprentices with valuable practice in aircraft disassembly and reassembly.** via HAAA

Above: **Hunter F.4 WV266/7781M was previously allocated to 234 Squadron before its arrival at Halton as an instructional aircraft.** Author

Left: **Javelin FAW.7 XH783/7798M, looking rather sorry for itself at Halton in the mid-1960s before final scrapping.** MAP

Below right: **The first of Halton's Vulcans was XA892, the fourth production B.1; it is seen here in 1962.** MAP

Below left: **Halton's second Vulcan was XA898/7856M which arrived in mid-1964 and was scrapped in 1971.** Author

Above: **Javelin FAW.1 7619M, the former XA560, was used for Armstrong-Siddeley engine development trials at Bitteswell, with the Sapphire Sa7 engine with reheat.** MAP

Top: **Canberra T.4 WJ878 saw a varied career before it was flown to Halton on 10th May 1960. It later became 7636M. Note in the background the Bellman hangar which was demolished and replaced with a modern structure in the early 1970s.** C F E Smedley

Right: **For many years, the Halton Glider Flight, equipped with the Slingsby T-21B Sedbergh TX.1, provided opportunities for gliding instruction to solo standard.** Author

Halton: The 1960s

Top left: **Activities of the Halton Society included the practical assembly of electronic circuits.** via HAAA

Top right: **The Halton Society did much to expand the horizons of apprentices. In this case, a group of apprentices of the 113th Entry visit the 24-hour race at Le Mans in June 1969.** Author

Above: **A scene from Padre's Hour in the late 1960s. Halton also took care of apprentices' spiritual welfare as it supervised the transition from youth to adult.** via HAAA

Left: **Aeromodelling was a well-supported activity of the Halton Society, as typified by this exhibit at an RAF display in the 1960s.** via HAAA

Left: **Former members of the pipe band come together again on 1st August 1970, for the 50th anniversary celebrations.** Author

Above: **Halton's own air show, often promoted as a Motor Show, has provided the gymnastic display team with an excellent audience for many years. This is the 1971 team in action.** via HAAA

Left: **Halton's apprentices have appeared in the Royal Tournament at London's Earl's Court in many guises. Here, the band is seen in the early 1970s.** via HAAA

Top: **Canberra WD999/7387M arrived in November 1956 and in 1970 still carried the nose markings of 551 Wing, Gutersloh, its final unit before allocation to Halton being 103 Squadron.** Author

Left:: **Beagle 206 G-ASWJ/8449M was loaned to Halton by Rolls-Royce, where it is seen in June 1976. In 1993 the aircraft was taken to the Midland Aircraft Museum at Coventry.** MAP

Centre left: **Unlike the majority of its colleagues, this Hunter met a fiery end at Halton in 1970.** MAP

Bottom left: **Twin Pioneer XM961/7978M was a novel aircraft used for engine running instruction.** Author

Below: **Halton's own Spitfire, now wearing its correct serial number RW386, seen at the Halton Air Show in August 1972.** Author

Above: **Former RAF Transport Command Comet C.2 XK716/7858M starting to look a little forsaken in August 1972.** Author

Below: **Although no longer in use, the 'Cockpit Classroom' was still in good condition in August 1970 on the occasion of the 50th anniversary of the Apprentice Scheme.** Author

Top: **One of a number of Provost T.1s to see use at Halton for engine running training, WV493/7696M is seen at an open day on 29th June 1974.** Author

Above: **Jet Provost 8083/M/69 (ex-XM367), sports an unusual version of the M-number which was prevalent in 1969.** Author

Left: **Hunter F.4 XF308/7777M seen with its fin removed and main undercarriage retracted. What with removal of the fins on two adjacent Hunters, it is possible that this former 130 Sqn machine was in the process of being dismantled for delivery to Hawker Siddeley Aviation for resale overseas.** Author

Above: **One of many Hunter F.4s lined up for the occasion of the 50th anniversary of the Apprentice Scheme. The aircraft WV258/7779M last served with 54 Squadron before arrival at Halton in 1963.** Author

Above: **One of Halton's many Sea Vixens, XJ526/8145M, at Halton in 1974.** Author

Centre right: **Vulcans and Hunters typify the training aircraft fleet in 1970, in this case on the 1st August, the day of the 50th anniversary of the Apprentice Scheme.** Author

Right: **Argosy XP409/8221M was the first such aircraft to arrive at Halton. it is seen here on 29th June 1974.** Author

HALTON
THE 1980s

Above: **The Queen's Colour is handed over to be placed on the Altar prior to the service of Dedication for the 133rd Entry.** via HAAA

Left: **The Colour Party with the Queen's Colour for No.1 SofTT, on the occasion of the Passing Out Parade of the 133rd Entry on 24th March 1982.** via HAAA

Below: **The 133rd and supporting entries advance in review order on 24th March 1982.** via HAAA

Top: **Kittiwake G-AWGM at the Air Show in June 1984, nearing the end of its rebuild for use by the Halton Aero Club. Unfortunately, the aircraft was damaged in a heavy landing on 18th January 1986.** Author

Above: **Halton's current 'gate guardian' is Hunter F.6 XF527/8680M, which stands next to Station Headquarters and in sight of Main Point. Photographed in 1987.** Author

Right: **Lewis VI and Lewis VII on parade for the passing-out parade of the 142nd Entry on 15th October 1986.** via HAAA

Photographs on the opposite page:

Top left: **Over the years a number of helicopters have seen use at Halton, including Whirlwind HAR10 XP395/8674M, illustrated in June 1981.** Author

Top right: **After early difficulties, the Sea Vixens were integrated into airfield training. Seen here is XN707/8144M in 1984.** Author

Centre left: **Seen on display at the Halton Air Show in June 1984 is Sedbergh WG496 of the Halton Glider Flight, still providing air experience for trainees after 30 years.** Author

Centre right: **Despite the outflow of Hunter F.4s in the 1970s, a few, including WT746/ 7770M, were still in service in 1987.** Author

Bottom left: **Halton saw the return of Hunters in the workshops when the Tactical Weapons Units re-equipped with the Hawk. Photographed in 1987, XE597/8874M was a Mk.6A formerly operated by 79 Sqn/1TWU. Later all but the cockpit section of this aircraft was scrapped.** Author

Bottom right: **Gnat T.1 XR980/8622M in use for hydraulic system functional checks on the airfield in September 1987.** Author

Photographs on this page:

Top left: **Apprentices make use of the dual cockpits of a Gnat T.1.** via HAAA

Top right: **Grob G.102 Astir RAFGSA 884 of the Chiltern Gliding Club, seen at the Halton Air Show in June 1984, and prior to sale as BGA 3843.** Author

Below: **Gleaming in the September sun in 1987, the roof of Halton House is visible through the trees as a Bessonneau hangar and Argosy T.2 XP442/8454M carry out their training duties on the airfield.** Author

Above: **Jaguar XX746/8895M is typical of the recent upgrade of the training fleet. When seen here in September 1987, the aircraft was being used for weapon load training.** Author

Above: **Apprentices prepare Gnat T.1 XP511/8619M for engine runs on 22nd September 1987.** Author

Left: **Jet Provost T.3 XM362/8230M is possibly the most colourful member of the training fleet. The aircraft has had large elements of the skin removed from one side only to illustrate typical forms of aircraft construction. In addition to the use of colour to depict different aspects of its design, the aircraft is also painted in desert camouflage, as seen here in September 1987.** Author

Left: **The front of the Schools building, covered in Boston Ivy and looking resplendent in September 1992, in contrast to its stark image 70 years earlier. 'Schools' is named after Air Vice-Marshal A C Kermode, formerly a civilian instructor at Halton who later joined the Education Branch of the RAF.** Author

Left: **Whilst they may be functional, modern hangars hardly look as aesthetic as the Bessonneau. The modern structure replaced a wartime Bellman hangar in the early 1970s whilst the Bessonneau was in use by the Chilterns Gliding Club of the RAF GSA when this photograph was taken in September 1992.** Author

Left: **The modern airfield control building in 1992. It was built in 1987 and is barely a shadow of its predecessor which was demolished.** Author

Left: **The arrival of Jaguars also provided the opportunity to make use of their engines to teach the techniques of modern gas turbine engine deep strip and assembly.** via HAAA

Below: **Even without wings, a Jaguar can still provide considerable capability for training. Seen here on 26th September 1992 is Jaguar GR.1A XX966/8904M.** Author

Above: **More than half a century separates the design of the two temporary hangars seen here in September 1992. Will the modern Rubb hangar in the background still be in use in 50 years time like the First World War Bessonneau in the foreground?** Author

Above right: **Jaguar GR.1 XX746/8895M provides a fitting backdrop to a conversation between ex-apprentices at the September 1992 Tri-annual reunion of the Halton Aircraft Apprentices Association.** Author

Right: **The arrival of the Harrier GR.5 and GR.7 on the front-line saw the release of a number of GR.3s for training and other purposes. Wearing the colourful markings of 4 Squadron, XW768/9072M is seen here on 26th September 1992.** Author

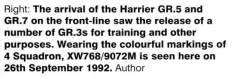

Right: **Following the introduction to service of the Tucano, Halton began to receive examples of the last model of the Jet Provost range, the T.5A. XW292/9128M, formerly with the RAF College, is seen at Halton in September 1992.** Author

Above: **Redundant Jet Provosts massed on the airfield in September 1992, pending a final decision on their disposal.** Author

Left: **With the planned phase-out of engineering training at Halton, already the training aircraft are being cleared out. Seen here in September 1992 is XS218/8508M, awaiting its fate.** Author

Below: **Whatever the future role of Halton, the Halton Spirit will live on. If any more reassurance were needed, then surely this scene on 26th September 1992, must give it. Many hundreds of ex-apprentices returned to Halton that day and a small proportion are seen here returning to the Wings to look over their former accommodation areas.** Author